How to Make Sense of Any Mess

Written & Illustrated By
Abby Covert

Edited By
Nicole Fenton

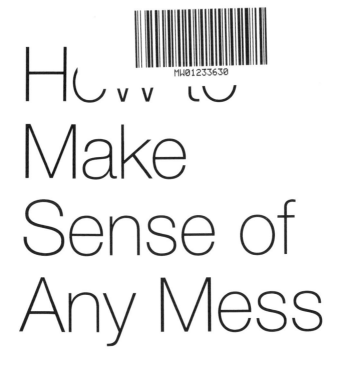

To Bill Pink, my grandfather, and the first information architect I ever knew. He taught me how rewarding it is to make sense of a mess.

"If you wish to make an apple pie from scratch,
you must first invent the universe."
– Carl Sagan, *Cosmos*

Introduction

Think about everything you have to make sense of each day... Projects, products, services, processes, collections, events, performances, boxes, drawers, closets, rooms, lists, plans, instructions, maps, recipes, directions, relationships, conversations, ideas...and the list goes on.

Having to progress in the face of chaos, confusion, and complexity is something we all have in common.

Information architecture is a set of concepts that can help anyone making anything to make sense of messes caused by misinformation, disinformation, not enough, or too much information.

Whether you're a student, teacher, designer, writer, technologist, analyst, business owner, marketer, director, or executive, this book is for you.

In the time that it takes to fly from New York to Chicago, I will introduce you to the practice of information architecture so you can start to make sense of whatever messes come your way.

About

Chapters: This book outlines a step-by-step process for making sense of messes made of information (and people). The steps are in order but most projects are not, so feel free to skip around or jump to a specific term from the lexicon.

Pages: Each page was conceived as a lesson in itself. The sequence is how I want to tell the story.

Characters: Each chapter ends with a story about a person who needs to make sense of a mess.

Worksheets: There are worksheets in each chapter to help you to make sense of your own messes. Each worksheet is simple enough to be easily recreated for your own purposes, but I have also provided links to print-ready templates on my website.

Indexed Lexicon: In the back of the book, you'll find a **lexicon** that defines and indexes the bolded terms in the book. The lexicon is also available online at: www.abbytheia.com/lexicon.

ISBN: 1500615994
ISBN-13: 978-1500615994

Contents

Change
Project
Chaos
Clutter
Complexity
Complicated
Disaster
Disorder
Mess
Cluster
Predicament
Quandary
Pickle
Situation
Nightmare

1

Identify
the Mess

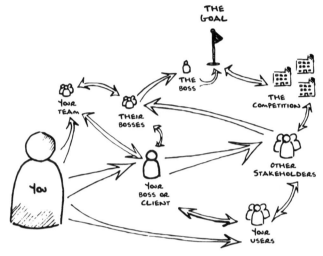

THE POLITICS of MAKING SENSE

Messes are made of information and people.

A **mess** is any situation where something is confusing or full of difficulty. We all encounter messes.

Here are some of the many messes we deal with in our everyday lives:

- The structure of teams and organizations

- The processes we undertake in working together

- The ways products and services are represented, sold, and delivered to us

- The ways we communicate with each other

It's hard to shine a light on the messes we face.

It's hard to be the one to say that something is a mess. Like a little kid standing at the edge of a dark room, we can be paralyzed by fear and not even know how to approach the mess.

These are the moments where confusion, procrastination, self-criticism, and frustration keep us from changing the world.

The first step to taming any mess is to shine a light on it so you can outline its edges and depths.

Once you brighten up your workspace, you can guide yourself through the complex journey of making sense of the mess.

I wrote this simple guidebook to help even the least experienced sensemakers tame the messes made of information (and people!) they're sure to encounter.

Information architecture is all around you.

Information architecture is the way that we arrange the parts of something to make it understandable.

Here are some examples of information architecture:

- Alphabetical cross-referencing systems used in a dictionary or encyclopedia

- Links in website navigation

- Sections, labels, and names of things on a restaurant menu

- Categories, labels and tasks used in a software program or application

- The signs that direct travelers in an airport

We rely on information architecture to help us make sense of the world around us.

Are you dealing with too much information, not enough information, or not the right information?

Things may change; the messes stay the same.

We've been learning how to architect information since the dawn of thought.

Page numbering, alphabetical order, indexes, lexicons, maps, and diagrams are all examples of information architecture achievements that happened well before the information age.

Even now, technology continues to change the things we make and use at a rate we don't understand yet. But when it really comes down to it, there aren't that many causes for confusing information.

A. Too much information

B. Not enough information

C. Not the right information

D. Some combination of these (eek!)

People architect information.

It's easy to think about information messes as if they're an alien attack from afar. But they're not.

We made these messes.

When we **architect** information, we determine the structures we need to communicate our message.

Everything around you was architected by another person. Whether or not they were aware of what they were doing. Whether or not they did a good job. Whether or not they delegated the task to a computer.

Information is a responsibility we all share.

We're no longer on the shore watching the information age approach; we're up to our hips in it.

If we're going to be successful in this new world, we need to see information as a workable material and learn to architect it in a way that gets us to our goals.

Every *thing* is complex.

Some things are simple. Some things are complicated. Every single *thing* in the universe is complex.

Complexity is part of the equation. We don't get to choose our way out of it.

Here are three complexities you may encounter:

- A common complexity is lacking a clear **direction** or agreeing on how to approach something you are working on with others.

- It can be complex to create, change, access, and maintain useful **connections** between people and systems, but these connections make it possible for us to communicate.

- People perceive what's going on around them in different ways. Differing **interpretations** can make a mess complex to work through.

Knowledge is complex.

Knowledge is surprisingly subjective.

We knew the earth was flat, until we knew it was *not flat*. We knew that Pluto was a planet until we knew it was *not a planet.*

True means without variation, but finding something that doesn't vary feels impossible.

Instead, to establish the truth, we need to confront messes without the fear of unearthing inconsistencies, questions, and opportunities for improvement. We need to be open to the variations of truth that are bound to exist.

Part of that includes agreeing on what things mean. That's our subjective truth. And it takes courage to unravel our conflicts and assumptions to determine what's actually true.

If other people have a different interpretation of what we're making, the mess can seem even bigger and more hairy. When this happens, we have to proceed with questions and set aside what we think we know.

Every *thing* has information.

Over your lifetime, you'll make, use, maintain, consume, deliver, retrieve, receive, give, consider, develop, learn, and forget many **things**.

This book is a thing. Whatever you're sitting on while reading is a thing. That thing you were thinking about a second ago? That's a thing too.

Things come in all sorts, shapes, and sizes.

The things you're making sense of may be analog or digital; used once or for a lifetime; made by hand or manufactured by machines.

I could have written a book about information architecture for websites or mobile applications or whatever else is trendy. Instead, I decided to focus on ways people could wrangle any mess, regardless of what it's made of.

That's because I believe every mess and every *thing* shares one important *non-thing*: information.

Information is whatever is conveyed or represented by a particular arrangement or sequence of things.

What's information?

Information is not a fad. It wasn't even invented in the information age. As a concept, information is old as language and collaboration is.

The most important thing I can teach you about information is that it isn't a *thing*. It's subjective, not objective. It's *whatever a user interprets* from the arrangement or sequence of things they encounter.

For example, imagine you're looking into a bakery case. There's one plate overflowing with oatmeal raisin cookies and another plate with a single double-chocolate chip cookie. Would you bet me a cookie that there used to be more double-chocolate chip cookies on that plate? Most people would take me up on this bet. Why? Because everything they already know tells them that there were probably more cookies on that plate.

The belief or non-belief that there were other cookies on that plate is the information each viewer *interprets* from the way the cookies were arranged. When we rearrange the cookies with the intent to change how people interpret them, we're architecting information.

While we can arrange things with the intent to communicate certain information, we can't actually *make* information. Our users do that for us.

Information is not data or content.

Data is facts, observations, and questions about something. **Content** can be cookies, words, documents, images, videos, or whatever you're arranging or sequencing.

The difference between information, data, and content is tricky, but the important point is that the absence of content or data can be just as *informing* as the presence.

For example, if we ask two people why there is an empty spot on a grocery store shelf, one person might interpret the spot to mean that a product is sold-out, and the other might interpret it as being popular.

The jars, the jam, the price tags, and the shelf are the content. The detailed observations each person makes about these things are data. What each person encountering that shelf believes to be true about the empty spot is the information.

Information is architected to serve different needs.

If you rip out the content from your favorite book and throw the words on the floor, the resulting pile is not your favorite book.

If you define each word from your favorite book and organize the definitions alphabetically, you would have a dictionary, not your favorite book.

If you arrange each word from your favorite book by gathering similarly defined words, you have a thesaurus, not your favorite book.

Neither the dictionary nor the thesaurus is anything like your favorite book, because both the architecture and the content determine how you interpret and use the resulting information.

For example, "8 of 10 Doctors Do Not Recommend" and "Doctor Recommended" are both true statements, but each serves a different intent.

Users are complex.

User is another word for a person. But when we use that word to describe someone else, we're likely implying that they're using the thing we're making. It could be a website, a product or service, a grocery store, a museum exhibit, or anything else people interact with.

When it comes to our use and interpretation of things, people are complex creatures.

We're full of contradictions. We're known to exhibit strange behaviors. From how we use mobile phones to how we traverse grocery stores, none of us are exactly the same. We don't know why we do what we do. We don't really know why we like what we like, but we do know it when we see it. We're fickle.

We expect things to be *digital*, but also, in many cases, *physical*. We want things to feel *auto-magic* while retaining a *human touch*. We want to be *safe*, but not *spied on*. We use words at our whim.

Most importantly perhaps, we realize that for the first time ever, we have easy access to other people's experiences to help us decide if something is worth experiencing at all.

Stakeholders are complex.

A **stakeholder** is someone who has a viable and legitimate interest in the work you're doing. Our stakeholders can be partners in business, life, or both.

Managers, clients, coworkers, spouses, family members, and peers are common stakeholders.

Sometimes we choose our stakeholders; other times, we don't have that luxury. Either way, understanding our stakeholders is crucial to our success. When we work against each other, progress comes to a halt.

Working together is difficult when stakeholders see the world differently than we do.

But we should expect opinions and personal preferences to affect our progress. It's only human to consider options and alternatives when we're faced with decisions.

Most of the time, there is no right or wrong way to make sense of a mess. Instead, there are many ways to choose from. Sometimes we have to be the one without opinions and preferences so we can weigh all the options and find the best way forward for everyone involved.

To do is to know.

Knowing is not enough. Knowing too much can encourage us to procrastinate. There's a certain point when continuing to *know* at the expense of doing allows the mess to grow further.

Practicing information architecture means exhibiting the courage to push past the edges of your current reality. It means asking questions that inspire change. It takes honesty and confidence in other people.

Sometimes, we have to move forward knowing that other people tried to make sense of this mess and failed. We may need to shine the light brighter or longer than they did. Perhaps now is a better time. We may know the outcomes of their fate, but we don't know our own yet. We can't until we try.

What if turning on the light reveals that the room is full of scary trolls? What if the light reveals the room is actually empty? Worse yet, what if turning on the light makes us realize we've been living in darkness?

The truth is that these are all potential realities, and understanding that is part of the journey. The only way to know what happens next is to do it.

Meet Carl.

Carl is a design student getting ready to graduate. But first, he has to produce a book explaining his design work and deliver a ten-minute presentation.

While Carl is a talented designer, public speaking makes him queasy and he doesn't consider himself much of a writer. He has drawers and boxes full of notes, scribbles, sketches, magazine clippings, quotes, and prototypes.

Carl has the pieces he needs to make his book and presentation come to life. He also has a momentum-killing fear of the mess he's facing.

To help Carl identify his mess, we could start by asking questions about its edges and depths:

- Who are his users and what does he know about them already? How could he find out more?

- Who are the stakeholders and what does he know about what they are expecting?

- How does he want people to interpret the work? What content would help that interpretation?

- What might distract from that interpretation?

It's your turn.

···

This chapter outlines why it's important to identify the edges and depths of a mess, so you can lessen your anxiety and make progress.

I also introduced the need to look further than what is true, and pay attention to how users and stakeholders interpret language, data, and content.

To start to identify the mess you're facing, work through these questions:

- Users: Who are your intended users? What do you know about them? How can you get to know them better? How might they describe this mess?

- Stakeholders: Who are your stakeholders? What are their expectations? What are their thoughts about this mess? How might they describe it?

- Information: What interpretations are you dealing with? What information is being created through a lack of data or content?

- Current state: Are you dealing with too much information, not enough information, not the right information, or a combination of these?

···

Draw your mess.

DRAW WHAT YOUR MESS
LOOKS LIKE TO YOU

WHAT WORDS WOULD USERS
AND STAKEHOLDERS USE TO
DESCRIBE YOUR MESS

_____   _____   _____

_____   _____   _____

_____   _____   _____

Download the worksheet at:
www.abbytheia.com/worksheets/mess.pdf

Goal
Bent
Wish
Impulse
Success
Good
Purpose
Intent
Daydream
Ambition
Aspiration
Point
Objective
Desire
Wants

2

State
Your Intent

Intent is language.

Intent is the effect we want to have on something. We make language-based decisions whenever we talk about our intent.

Our language choices change how we use our time and energy. For every word we use to describe where we want to go, there's another word that we're walking away from.

For every *amusement park* you make, you're not making a *video game*. When you intend to be fun for *kids*, you can use *stories* but not *metaphors*. If you want something to be *relaxing*, it's harder to make it *educational*.

The words we choose matter. They represent the ideas we want to bring into the world.

We need words so we can make plans. We need words to turn ideas into things.

For example, if we say that we want to make *sustainable eco-centered design solutions*, we can't rely on thick, glossy paper catalogs to help us reach new customers. By choosing those words, we completely changed our options.

What is *good?*

Language is any system of communication that exists to establish shared meaning. Even within a single language, one term can mean something in situation A and something different in situation B. We call this a **homograph**. For example, the word *pool* can mean a swimming pool, shooting pool, or a betting pool.

Perception is the process of considering, and interpreting something. Perception is subjective like truth is. Something that's beautiful to one person may be an eyesore to another. For example, many designers would describe the busy, colorful patterns in the carpets of Las Vegas as *gaudy*. People who frequent casinos often describe them as *beautiful*.

However *good* or *bad* these carpet choices seem to us, there are reasons why they look that way. Las Vegas carpets are busy and colorful to disguise spills and wear and tear from foot traffic. Gamblers likely enjoy how they look because of an association with an activity that they enjoy. For Las Vegas casino owners and their customers, those carpet designs are good. For designers, they're bad. Neither side is right. Both sides have an opinion.

What we intend to do determines how we define words like *good* and *bad*.

Good is in the eye of the beholder.

What's good for a business of seven years may not work for a business of seven weeks. What works for one person may be destructive for another.

When we don't define what *good* means for our stakeholders and users, we aren't using language to our advantage. Without a clear understanding of what is good, bad can come out of nowhere.

And while you have to define what good means to create *good* information architecture, it's not just the architecture part that needs this kind of focus.

Every decision you make should support what you've defined as good: from the words you choose to the tasks you enable, and everything in between.

When you're making decisions, balance what your stakeholders and users expect of you, along with what they believe to be good.

Looking good versus *being* good.

Pretty things can be useless, and ugly things can be useful. Beauty and quality are not always related.

When making things, we should aim to give equal attention to looking good and being good. If either side of that duality fails, the whole suffers.

As users, we may assume that a good-looking thing will also be useful and well thought-out. But it only takes a minute or two to see if our assumptions are correct. If it isn't good, we'll know.

As sensemakers, we may fall victim to these same assumptions about the relationships between beauty and quality of thought.

Beware of pretty things. Pretty things can lie and hide from reality. Ugly things can too.

If we're going to sort out the messes around us, we need to ask difficult questions and go deeper than how something looks to determine if it's good or not.

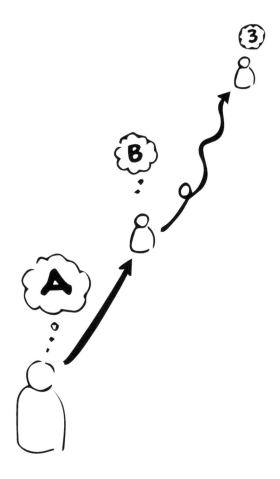

How many times has your intended meaning been distorted while moving through a messy human network?

Meaning can get lost in translation.

Did you ever play the telephone game as a child?

It consists of a group of kids passing a phrase down the line in a whisper. The point of the game is to see how messed up the meaning of the initial message becomes when sent across a messy human network.

Meaning can get lost in subtle ways. It's wrapped up in perception, so it's also subjective. Most misunderstandings stem from mixed up meanings and miscommunication of messages.

Miscommunications can lead to disagreements and frustration, especially when working with others.

Getting our message across is something everyone struggles with. To avoid confusing each other, we have to consider how our message could be interpreted.

Who matters?

The meaning we intend to communicate doesn't matter if it makes no sense, or the wrong sense, to the people we want to reach.

We need to consider our intended users. Sometimes they're our customers or the public. Often times, they're also stakeholders, colleagues, employees, partners, superiors, or clients. These are the people who use our process.

To determine who matters, ask these questions:

- Who's most important to get agreement from?

- Who's most important to serve?

- What words might make them defensive?

- What words might put them at ease?

- How open are they to change?

- How will this affect their lives?

- How does the current state of things look to them? Is that good or bad?

Start with *why.*

Understanding the **why** behind what you're making allows you to uncover your intent and potential.

When everyone knows why they're doing something, the way forward is clearer and each person can understand their individual responsibilities.

Having a strong *why* will get you further. Having a weak *why* won't make it any easier to get up in the morning. Your *why* should be part of everything you do, not just your mission statement.

Why? Because without a clear reason for doing something, even the most committed and loyal person will eventually abandon the hope of finishing the task.

To start with *why*, ask yourself:

- Why does this work need to be done?

- Why is change needed? Why do those changes matter? Why should other people care?

- Why hasn't this been tackled correctly?

- Why will this time be different?

What before *how.*

There are reasons it makes sense to wait to cook until after you know what you're making. For these same reasons, we all know not to construct a building without a plan.

When we jump into a task without thinking about **what** we're trying to accomplish, we can end up with solutions to the wrong problem. We can waste energy that would be better spent determining which direction to take.

When deciding what you're doing, ask yourself:

- What are you trying to change? What is your vision for the future? What is within your abilities?

- What do you know about the quality of what exists today? What further research will help you understand it?

- What has been done before? What can you learn from those experiences? What is the market and competition like? Has anyone succeeded or failed at this in the past?

How varies widely.

The saying "there are many ways to skin a cat" reminds us that we have options when it comes to achieving our intent. There are many ways to do just about anything.

Whether you're working on a museum exhibit, a news article, or a grocery store, you should explore all of your options before choosing a direction.

How is an ever-growing list of directions we *could* take while staying true to our reasons *why*.

To look at your options, ask yourself:

- How could we communicate our message?

- How much time and effort will it take?

- How could the solution look and feel?

- How will this be produced?

- How will this be maintained?

- How will this be measured?

- How will we know if we've succeeded?

Why, *what*, and *how* are deeply interrelated.

Our why, what, and how aren't always determined in a linear process. The answers to these fundamental questions may change from moment to moment.

Your *why* may be "because you want this checked off your to-do list" or "because you want to play with certain materials or ideas."

Your resulting *what* might be to "start making the first thing that comes to mind."

They may not be lofty in intent, but the intent has been stated. These are valid answers to *why* and *what* that will serve as a guide for *how* you define what is good. Your actions will be the result of your answers.

How long would you spend on a task without understanding why it's important or what you are actually accomplishing? Constantly answering these basic questions are a big part of our everyday life.

Language is the material of intent.

The words we choose change the things we make and how we think about them. Our words also change how other people make sense of our work.

In writing this book, my intent was to make it:

- Accessible

- Beginner-friendly

- Useful in a broad range of situations

As a result, I had to be comfortable with it not being these other things:

- Academic

- Expert-friendly

- Useful in specific situations

Meet Karen.

Karen is a product manager at a startup. Her CEO thinks the key to launching their product in a crowded market is a *sleek* look and feel.

Karen recently conducted research to test the product with its intended users. With the results in hand, she worries that what the CEO sees as *sleek* is likely to seem *cold* to the users they want to reach.

Karen has research on her side, but she still needs to define what *good* means for her organization. Her team needs to state their intent.

To establish an intent, Karen talks with her CEO about how their users' aesthetic wants don't line up with the look and feel of the current product.

She starts their conversation by confirming that the users from her research are part of the intended audience for the product.

Next, she helps the CEO create a list of questions and actions the research brought up.

Afterwards, Karen develops a plan for communicating her findings to the rest of the team.

State your intent.

Like Karen, you need to make sure the language you use to state your intent doesn't stand in your way. The following exercise will help you state your intent and clarify your language with other people.

- First, choose a set of adjectives you want your users to use to describe what you're making.

- Then, choose a set of adjectives that you're okay with not being used to describe the same thing.

I find these rules helpful during this exercise:

- When put together, each set of words should neither repeat nor disagree with each other. The second set shouldn't be a list of opposites from the first.

- Avoid negative adjectives, like slow or bad or ugly. Keep each word as neutral as possible. A good test is that someone shouldn't be able to tell which list is positive or negative.

Choose your words.

IDEALLY MY WORK WOULD
BE DESCRIBED BY USERS AS:

_____

_____

_____

THAT MEANS, MY WORK
WILL NOT BE DESCRIBED AS:

_____

_____

_____

Download the worksheet at:
abbytheia.com/worksheets/intent.pdf

Fact
Opinion
Experience
Perception
Emotion
Possibility
Truth
Reality
Subjectivity
Life
Actuality
Money
Environment
Materials
Context

3

Face
Reality

By facing reality, we can find solutions.

Whenever we're making something, there are moments when it's no longer time to ponder. It's time to act, to make, to realize, and perhaps to fail.

Fear is an obvious but elusive partner in these moments. Fear can walk ahead of us and get all the glory, leaving us pondering and restless for more, more, more. Maybe we fear failure. Maybe we fear success. Maybe we fear light being shined our way.

Confronting your fears and knowing what is real is an important part of making sense of a mess.

Facing **reality** is the next step on our journey. In this chapter, we'll discuss rabbit holes of reality you are likely to have to explore as well as some diagrammatic techniques you can take with you to document what you find down there.

Before we go on, I have to warn you of the many opportunities ahead to lose faith in yourself as you climb through and understand the details of your reality. It can start to feel like the mess wants you to fail in making sense of it. Don't worry. That thought has occurred to everyone who has ever tried to change something. We all have to deal with reality. We all want what we want and then get what we get.

Reality involves many players.

As you go through the mess, you'll encounter several types of players:

- Current users: People who interact with whatever you're making.

- Potential users: People you hope to reach.

- Stakeholders: People who care about the outcome of what you're making.

- Competitors: People who share your current or potential users.

- Distractors: People that could take attention away from your intent.

You may play several of these roles yourself. Be aware of potential conflicts there.

For example, if you believe your users are like you but they're not, there's more room for incorrect assumptions and miscommunications.

Reality involves many factors.

No matter what you're making, you probably need to consider several of these factors:

- Time: "I only have _____."

- Resources: "I have _____."

- Skillset: "I know how to _____ , but I don't know how to _____ yet."

- Environment: "I'm working in a _____."

- Personality: "I want this work to say _____ about me."

- Politics: "Others want this work to say _____ about _____."

- Ethics: "I want this work to do right by the world by _____."

- Integrity: "I want to be proud of the results of my work, which means _____."

Reality happens across channels and contexts.

A **channel** transmits information. A commercial on TV and YouTube is accessible on two channels. A similar message could show up in your email inbox, on a billboard, on the radio, or in the mail.

We live our lives across channels.

It's common to see someone using a smartphone while sitting in front of a computer screen, or reading a magazine while watching TV.

As users, our **context** is the situation we're in, including where we are, what we're trying to do, how we're feeling, and anything else that shapes our experience. Our context is always unique to us and can't be relied upon to hold steady.

If I'm tweeting about a TV show while watching it, my context is "sitting on my couch, excited enough about what I'm watching to share my reactions."

In this context, I'm using several different channels: Twitter, a smartphone, and TV.

Reality has many intersections.

Tweeting while watching TV is an example of two channels working together to support a single context.

A single channel can also support multiple contexts. For example, a website may serve someone browsing on a phone from their couch, on a tablet at a café, or on a desktop computer in a cubicle.

When you begin to unravel a mess, it's easy to be overwhelmed by the amount of things that need to come together to support even the simplest of contexts gracefully on a single channel.

"It's just a _____" is an easy trap to fall into. But to make sense of real-world problems, you need to understand how users, channels, and context relate to each other.

What channels do your users prefer? What context are they likely in when encountering what you're making? How are they feeling? Are they in a hurry? Are they on slow Wi-Fi? Are they there for entertainment or to accomplish a task?

Considering these small details will make a huge difference for you and your users.

Reality doesn't always fit existing patterns.

Beware of jumping into an existing solution or copying existing patterns. In my experience, too many people buy into an existing solution's flexibility to later discover its rigidity.

Imagine trying to design a luxury fashion magazine using a technical system for grocery store coupons. The features you need may seem similar enough until you consider your context. That's when reality sets in.

What brings whopping returns to one business might crush another. What works for kids might annoy older people. What worked five years ago may not work today.

We have to think about the effects of adopting an existing structure or language before doing so.

When architecting information, focus on your own unique objectives. You can learn from and borrow from other people. But it's best to look at their decisions through the lens of your intended outcome.

OBJECT

How many times have you been in a discussion where a picture would have been worth a thousand words?

Objects let us have deeper conversations about reality.

When you discuss a specific subject, you subconsciously reference part of a large internal map of what you know.

Other people can't see this map. It only exists in your head, and it's called your **mental model.**

When faced with a problem, you reference your mental model and try to organize the aspects and complexities of what you see into recognizable patterns. Your ongoing experience changes your mental model. This book is changing it right now.

We create **objects** like maps, diagrams, prototypes, and lists to share what we understand and perceive. Objects allow us to compare our mental models with each other.

These objects represent our ideas, actions, and insights. When we reference objects during a conversation, we can go deeper and be more specific than verbalizing alone.

As an example, it's much easier to teach someone about the inner-workings of a car engine with a picture, animation, diagram, or working model.

Who is the object for, and how will it be used?

Start with scope and scale.

Before you make objects like diagrams or maps, spend some time determining their scope and scale.

Scope is your clearly stated purpose for the diagram. The scope of a blueprint for an actual house is greater than the scope of a diagram explaining the rooms that make up a typical house.

Scale is the relative size of your diagrammatic work. The scale of a map covering a wall is greater than the scale of a map on regular-sized paper.

To think through scope and scale, ask yourself:

• What do people need to understand?

• What are the edges of the map or diagram?

• What are you not mapping or diagramming?

• Where will other people see this map or diagram (e.g., on a wall, in a presentation, on paper)?

Timescale matters.

While you're thinking about scope and scale, consider the timescale you're working with.

A **timescale** is a period of time your map or diagram represents. There are three main timescales:

- Then: How did things used to be?

- Now: How are things today?

- When: How do you see it being in the future?

It's often easier to think about how things were then or how they are now before proposing changes.

As an example, if we wanted to make sense of changes to the American healthcare system over the last year, we could diagram at each of the three timescales:

- Then: How did healthcare work ten years ago?

- Now: How does healthcare work today?

- When: How do we want health care to work after we've made these changes?

Reality involves many players.

Rhetoric is communication designed to have a persuasive effect on its audience.

Here are some common rhetorical reasons for making diagrams and maps:

- Reflection: Point to a future problem (e.g., a map of a local landfill's size in the past, present, and projected future).

- Options: Show something as it could be (e.g., a diagram showing paths a user could take to set up an application).

- Improvements: Show something as it should be (e.g., a diagram pointing out opportunities found during user research).

- Identification: Show something as it once was or is today (e.g., a map of your neighborhood).

- Plan: Show something as it will be (e.g., a map of your neighborhood with bike lanes).

ONE-WAY RELATIONSHIP:

TWO-WAY RELATIONSHIP:

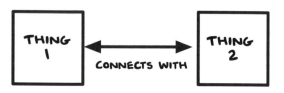

LOGIC-BASED RELATIONSHIP:

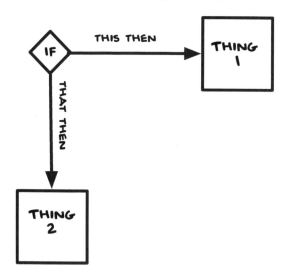

Architecture before design.

You can tell complex stories in a diagram with boxes and arrows. A box represents a thing; an arrow represents a **relationship** between things.

These relationships can be one-way (e.g., dropping a package into a mailbox) or two-way (e.g., calling the postal service to see if it was delivered).

We use a diamond shape to represent a decision point. This allows us to diagram relationships that change depending on the circumstances.

When you're making a diagram, keep the structure pliable. Give yourself room to play with the boxes, move them around, and see what happens.

Start by creating a box for each concept, each piece of content, and each process. Arrange the boxes based on how they relate to each other. Play. See what reveals itself as you move things around. Try a few different arrangements before you add the arrows.

Keep it simple. The more you add styling and polish, the less you'll feel comfortable changing and collaborating on the diagram.

Keep it tidy.

If people judge books by their covers, they judge diagrams by their tidiness.

People use aesthetic cues to determine how legitimate, trustworthy, and useful information is. Your job is to produce a tidy representation of what you're trying to convey without designing it too much or polishing it too early in the process.

As you make your diagram, keep your stakeholders in mind. Will they understand it? Will anything distract them? Crooked lines, misspellings, and styling mistakes lead people astray. Be careful not to add another layer of confusion to the mess.

Make it easy to make changes so you can take in feedback quickly and keep the conversation going, rather than defending or explaining the diagram.

Your diagram ultimately needs to be tidy enough for stakeholders to understand and comment on it, while being flexible enough to update.

Expand your toolbox.

Objects like diagrams, maps, and charts aren't one-size-fits-all. Play with them, adapt them, and expand on them for your own purposes.

The biggest mistake I see beginner sensemakers make is not expanding their toolbox of diagrammatic and mapping techniques.

There are thousands, maybe millions, of variations on the form, quality, and testing of diagrams and maps. And more are being created and experimented with each day.

The more diagrams you get to know, the more tools you have. The more ways you can frame the mess, the more likely you are to see the way through to the other side.

To help you build your toolbox, I've included ten diagrams and maps I use regularly in my own work.

As you review each one, imagine the parts of your mess that could benefit from reframing.

1. Block Diagram

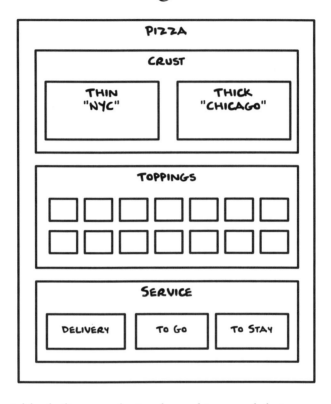

A **block diagram** depicts how objects and their attributes interrelate to create a concept.

A **concept** is an abstract idea or general notion that exists in people's mental models. For example, pizza is a concept on which many actual pies are fired.

2. Flow Diagram

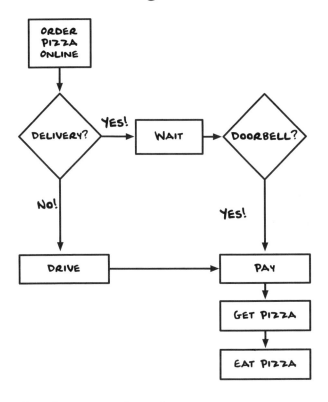

A **flow diagram** outlines the steps in a process, including conditions a user or system is under, and connections between tasks.

Conditions are rules that dictate the flow. For example, the path I take in the flow is different if I'm ordering for pickup or delivery.

3. Gantt Chart

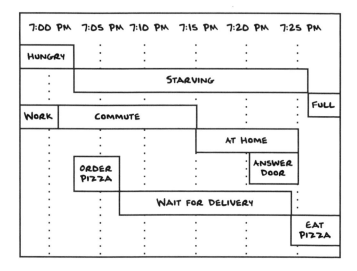

A **Gantt chart** depicts how processes relate to one another over time. Timelines, and project plans are both common examples of Gantt charts.

This type of chart helps us to understand relationships between people, tasks, and time.

4. Quadrant Diagram

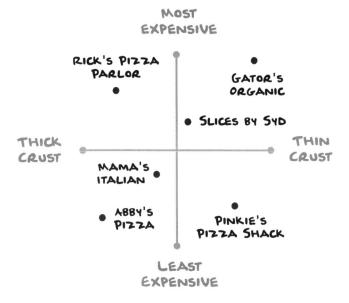

MOST
EXPENSIVE

RICK'S PIZZA
PARLOR

GATOR'S
ORGANIC

SLICES BY SYD

THICK
CRUST

THIN
CRUST

MAMA'S
ITALIAN

ABBY'S
PIZZA

PINKIE'S
PIZZA SHACK

LEAST
EXPENSIVE

A **quadrant diagram** illustrates how things compare to one another. You can create one based on exact data (e.g., price of a slice, thickness of pizza-crust) or ambiguous data (e.g., fancy or casual, quality of service, or tastiness).

This diagram would be more exact with prices and crust measurements. (But how do you properly measure the thickness of pizza crust anyways?)

5. Venn Diagram

A **Venn diagram** is useful for highlighting overlapping concepts or objects. The overlap, known to some as the hedgehog or the nut, represents how these things relate. In this example, both pizza and movie relate to Friday night at home.

This same technique can be used to sort things into sets based on how they're similar. For example, we might make a circle for movies we love and one for movies referencing pizza, and put the movies we love that reference pizza in the overlap.

6. Swim Lane Diagram

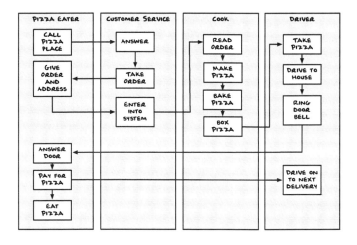

A **swim lane diagram** depicts how multiple players work together to complete a task or interact within a process. The result is a list of tasks for each user. This is especially useful when you're trying to understand how different teams or people work together.

7. Hierarchy Diagram

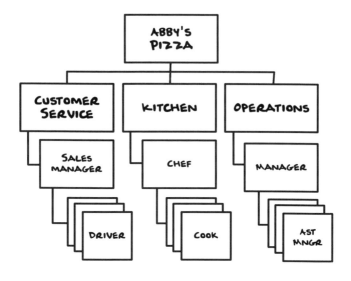

A **hierarchy diagram** depicts how objects, concepts, people, and places relate to each other. In website design, hierarchy diagrams are often called **sitemaps.**

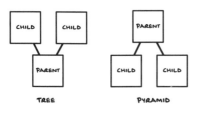

L-brackets, as seen above, tend to be easiest to read, but you may also see hierarchical relationships depicted as trees or pyramids.

8. Mind Map

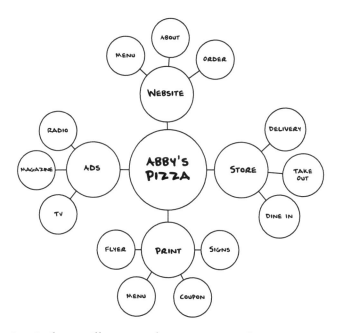

A **mind map** illustrates the connections between concepts, objects, ideas, channels, people, and places within a particular context.

These concepts don't necessarily live under an established hierarchy or sequence. For example, in the diagram above, I've outlined the various aspects of running a pizza parlor as the owner (me!) might think about them.

9. Schematic

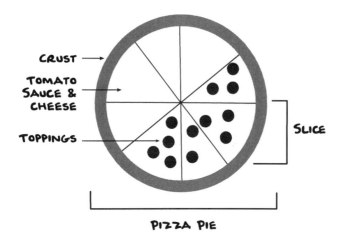

PIZZA PIE

A **schematic** is a diagram of an object or interface simplified for the sake of clarity. Schematics are known by many other names including wireframes, sketches, lo-fis, and blueprints.

Since a schematic reduces complexity, unintended errors and ambiguity can be introduced. Would someone understand from the previous schematic to put cheese on top of the tomato sauce? Maybe not.

This is a case where an **exploded schematic** is useful, because it shows how the individual pieces come together to form the whole.

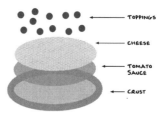

10. Journey Map

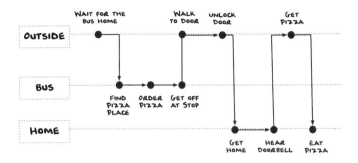

A **journey map** shows all of the steps and places that make up a person or group's experience.

The rows represent the user's context (e.g., outside, on the bus, at home). Each point represents an event or a task that makes up the overall journey. Each point is placed sequentially as it relates to the other points.

This example shows events that only involve one person, but journey maps are also useful for showing the movement of pairs, teams, and organizations.

Try diagramming.

1. Make a block diagram that shows how the pieces of a concept interrelate.

2. Demystify a process by making a flow diagram.

3. Break your latest project down into its individual tasks and make a Gantt chart.

4. Compare a group of restaurants in your neighborhood in a quadrant diagram.

5. Explore what happens when concepts or objects overlap using a Venn diagram.

6. Break any multi-user process into a list of tasks per user with a swim lane diagram.

7. Depict the content and organization of your favorite website in a hierarchy diagram.

8. Unload all of the cool ideas in your mind right now in a mind map.

9. Explain how to make your favorite food with a simple schematic. Bonus point for exploding it!

10. Make a journey map of a day in your life.

Meet Maggie.

Maggie is the creative director for a small agency. She has a new client, and doesnt understand their business.

She reads their website, annual reports, and printed brochures, and still can't pinpoint what they do. She's not the only one. It turns out that no one on her team can figure out what the client's business does either. Maggie knows she has to clear this up before overseeing work for the client.

Even if Maggie is the most talented creative director in the world, her work won't matter much until she faces the reality that she doesn't understand her client's business. She needs to get a clearer mental model out of her client's head and into her team's hands.

In an attempt to face reality, Maggie asks her client to describe the business in the simplest way possible. "Like you would at a grade school career day," she says.

With that as a basic model, she can ask better questions and compare her client's mental model with her own. She uses a mind map to capture thoughts as they talk. After talking with her client, Maggie has a clearer understanding of their business and much more confidence that her team can support their needs.

Face your reality.

Everything is easier with a map. Let me guide you through making a map for your own mess.

On the following page is another favorite diagram of mine, the **matrix diagram**.

The power of a matrix diagram is that you can make the boxes collect whatever you want. Each box becomes a task to fulfill or a question to answer, whether you're alone or in a group.

Matrix diagrams are especially useful when you're facilitating a discussion, because they're easy to create and they keep themselves on track. An empty box means you're not done yet.

After making a simple matrix of users, contexts, players, and channels, you'll have a guide to understanding the mess. By admitting your hopes and fears, you're uncovering the limits you're working within.

This matrix should also help you understand the other diagrams and objects you need to make, along with who will use and benefit from them.

Diagram your reality.

CONTRIBUTING FACTORS

| WHO ARE YOUR STAKEHOLDERS? | WHO ARE YOUR DISTRACTORS? |

| WHAT DO YOU KNOW ABOUT YOUR USERS? | IN WHAT CONTEXT ARE USERS LIKELY IN? |

WHERE MIGHT YOU BEST SERVE USERS? (EXAMPLES: A MOBILE APPLICATION, A WEBSITE, BY MAIL, IN PERSON)

LIMITING FACTORS

| WHAT ARE YOU MOST FEARFUL OF? | WHAT ARE YOU MOST HOPEFUL ABOUT? |

Download the worksheet at:
abbytheia.com/worksheets/reality.pdf

Way
Choice
Flavor
Type
Decision
Determination
Direction
Orders
Steering
Turning
Guide
Course
Trajectory

4

Choose a Direction

Moving from *why* to *what*.

After you face reality, it still takes a tremendous amount of work and courage to move from understanding *why* something needs to change to knowing *what* you can do about it.

There are many directions to choose from. Each has its own twists and turns.

People often get in their own way by becoming overwhelmed with choices, choosing not to choose instead. Others are limited by frustration over things they can't change immediately or easily.

Change takes time.

Start by choosing a direction to go toward. If you take one step in that direction each day, you'll get to the finish line in due time.

If you spend all your time thinking about how far the finish line is and fearing never getting there, you'll make slower progress or never make it at all.

We work at different levels.

When we reference a place, it exists within other places. If I say, "I live in SoHo," that place is within another place called Manhattan, which is within a place called New York City.

When we reference *things*, they exist within other things and places too. For example, a mug exists within a cabinet, in a coffee shop, in a building, on a city block, in a neighborhood, in a city, in a state, in a country, on a continent, and so on.

Digital things live within other things and places, including physical and analog places. For example, a user accesses a mobile application on a smartphone, in a coffee shop, in a building, on a city block…

We make places and we make things. The places and things that we make are part of a user's real life.

What *are* you making?

Nothing exists in a vacuum. Everything connects to a larger whole. Whenever you're making something, figure out which levels you're working at:

 Object: a specific thing.

 Interface: a point where a user affects that thing.

 Location: a particular place or position.

 Journey: the steps in or between locations.

 Structure: a configuration of objects and locations.

 System: a set of structures working together.

 Ecosystem: a collection of related systems.

These levels deeply affect one another.

Once you know what level you're working at, you can zoom in to the appropriate level of detail. Sometimes we need to zoom all the way in on an object. Other times it's more important to zoom out to look at the ecosystem. Being able to zoom in and out as you work is the key to seeing how these levels affect one another.

When you're deep in the details, it's easy to forget your broad effect. When you're working overhead, it's easy to forget how your decisions affect things down on the ground. Making changes at one level without considering the affects they have on other levels can lead to friction and dissatisfaction between our users, our stakeholders, and us. One tiny change can spark a thousand disruptions.

For example, if we owned a restaurant and decided to eliminate paper napkins to be environmentally friendly, that would impact the entire restaurant, not just the table service our diners experience.

We'd need to consider other factors like where dirty napkins go, how we collect them, how often they're picked up and cleaned, how many napkins we need on hand between cleanings, and if we should use paper napkins if something spills in the dining room.

One tiny decision leads to another, and another.

We make places.

You can turn a space into a place by arranging it so people know what to do there. This act is called **placemaking**. If you arrange a table and chairs in the middle of a room, meetings, meals, study, and play are all potential uses of that place. But if you add a fancy dining set and linens to the table, you're suggesting that it's a dining area.

In placemaking, you **choreograph** a sequence of steps users can take and decide how you want them to move. You can recommend steps, but they'll move wherever and however they want. They may move the place settings aside and open a laptop for a meeting. You can prescribe the steps, but they do the dancing.

The ways you enforce your way of doing things changes how users think about the place you made and perhaps ultimately, how they think about you.

You could add a sign that says "Dining Only Please." You could also add waitstaff wearing tuxedos and glaring dispositions. Each of these would say something about you and the place you made.

The way we choose to arrange a place changes how people intrepret and use it. We encode our intent through the clues we leave for users to know what we want them to do.

There are spaces between the places we make.

When you're cleaning up a big mess, assess the spaces between places as well as the places themselves.

A **place** is a space designated for a specific purpose.

For example, if you built a public park, you might make a path to walk on, a picnic area, a playground, some bathrooms, and a soccer field. These areas were made with tasks in mind.

If parkgoers wear down a path through your fresh laid grass, you as the parkitect (ha!) could see it as an annoyance. Or you could see it as a space between places and pave over it so people can get where they want to go without walking through the mud.

A **space** is an open, free, or unoccupied area.

Space may not have a designated purpose yet, but that doesn't stop users from going there.

No matter what you're making, your users will find spaces between places. They bring their own context and channels with them, and they show you where you should go next. Find areas in flux and shine a light on them.

Language matters.

I once had a project where the word "asset" was defined three different ways across five teams.

I once spent three days defining the word "customer".

I once defined and documented over a hundred acronyms in the first week of a project for a large company, only to find 30 more the next week.

I wish I could say that I'm exaggerating or that any of this effort was unnecessary. Nope. Needed.

Language is complex. But language is also fundamental to understanding the direction we choose. Language is how we tell other people what we want, what we expect of them, and what we hope to accomplish together.

Without language, we can't collaborate.

Unfortunately, it's far too easy to declare a direction in language that doesn't make sense to those it needs to support: users, stakeholders, or both.

When we don't share a language with our users and our stakeholders, we have to work that much harder to communicate clearly.

Reduce linguistic insecurity.

The average person gives and receives directions all day long, constantly experiencing the impact of language and context. Whether it's a grocery list from a partner or a memo from a manager, we've all experienced what happens when a poor choice of words leads to the wrong outcome. Whether we're confused by one word or the entire message, the anxiety that comes from misunderstanding someone else's language is incredibly frustrating.

Imagine that on your first day at a new job every concept, process, and term you're taught is labeled with nonsense jargon. Now imagine the same first day, only everything you're shown has clear labels you can easily remember. Which second day would you want?

We can be insecure or secure about the language we're expected to use. We all prefer security.

Linguistic insecurity is the all too common fear that our language won't conform to the standard or style of our context.

To work together, we need to use language that makes sense to everyone involved.

Understand ontology.

If we were to write a dictionary, we'd be practicing **lexicography,** or collecting many meanings into a list. When we decide that a word or concept holds a specific meaning in a specific context, we are practicing **ontology.**

Here are some examples of ontological decisions:

- Social networks redefining "like" and "friends" for their purposes

- The "folders" on a computer's "desktop" you use to organize "files"

- The ability to order at a fast food chain by saying a number

To refine your ontology, all you need is a pile of sticky notes, a pen, and some patience.

1. Find a flat or upright surface to work on.

2. Write a term or concept that relates to your work on each sticky note.

3. Put the sticky notes onto the surface as they relate to each other. Start to create structures and relationships based on their location.

Your ontology already exists.

Ontology always exists, but the one you have today may be messy or nonsensical. If you were trying to understand the ontology of your grocery store, your map might look like this at first:

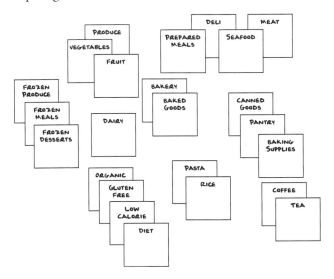

By asking your customers for words they think about within a grocery store, your map could grow to reflect overlapping and related terms.

If you were choosing words for the aisle and department signs or the website, this exercise would help you along.

Design *with*, not for.

It's important to discuss and vet your ontological decisions with stakeholders and users. Talking about language choices gives you a chance to test them.

It may sound obvious, but it's quite common to think something is clearly defined before talking about it with other people.

A good starting point in exploring ontology is to bring everyone together to make a list of terms and concepts. Ask each person to share:

- One term that they wish they knew more about

- One term that they wish others understood better

Go through each term as a group and use this as a forum for educating each other on what you know about language and context. Don't "uh huh" your way through words you've never heard or don't understand. Instead, untangle acronyms and unfamiliar phrases.

If someone uses a different word than you do, ask for clarification. Why do they use that word? Get them to explain it. Complexity tends to hide in minutiae.

Create a list of words you say.

A **controlled vocabulary** is an organized list of terms, phrases, and concepts intended to help someone navigate a specific context.

Documenting language standards can reduce linguistic insecurity.

A good controlled vocabulary considers:

- Variant spellings (e.g., American or British)

- Tone (e.g., *Submit* or *Send*)

- Scientific and popular terms (e.g., *cockroaches* or *Periplaneta Americana*)

- Insider and outsider terms (e.g., what we say at work; what we say in public)

- Acceptable synonyms (e.g., *automobile, car, auto*, or *vehicle*)

- Acceptable acronyms (e.g., *General Electric, GE*, or *G.E.*)

Create a list of words you *don't* say.

A controlled vocabulary doesn't have to end with terms you intend to use. Go deeper by defining terms and concepts that misalign with your intent.

For the sake of clarity, you can also define:

- Terms and concepts that conflict with a user's mental model of how things work

- Terms and concepts that have alternative meaning for users or stakeholders

- Terms and concepts that carry historical, political, or cultural baggage

- Acronyms and homographs that may confuse users or stakeholders

In my experience, a list of things you don't say can be even more powerful than a list of things you do. I've been known to wear a whistle and blow it in meetings when someone uses a term from the *don't* list.

Words I don't say in this book.

I've avoided using these terms and concepts:

1. Doing/Do the IA (commonly misstated)

2. IA (as an abbreviation)

3. Information Architecture (as a proper noun)

4. Information Architect (exceptions in my dedication and bio pages)

5. App as an abbreviation (too trendy)

6. Very (the laziest word ever)

7. User experience (too specific to design)

8. Metadata (too technical)

9. Semantic (too academic)

10. Semiotic (too academic)

I have reasons why these words aren't good in the context of this book. That doesn't mean I never use them; I do in some contexts.

Define terms for outsiders.

When I was in grade school, we did an assignment where we were asked to define terms clearly enough for someone learning our language. To define "tree" as "a plant that grows from the ground," we first needed to define "plant," "grow," and "ground."

It was an important lesson to start to understand the interconnectivity of language. I like to apply this kind of thinking in my work to uncover terms that are nested within other terms and their definitions.

To define a term clearly:

1. Write down the meaning of the term as simply as you can.

2. Underline each term within your definition that needs to be further defined.

3. Define those terms and test your definition with someone who doesn't know those terms yet.

4. Look at each individual word and ask yourself: What does this mean? Is it as simple as possible?

Understand the past.

As you talk through your controlled vocabulary, listen for stories and images people associate with each term.

Language has history. Synonyms and alternatives abound. Myths can get in your way too, unless you're willing to uncover them.

Gather the following about each term:

- History: How did the term come into being? How has it changed over time?

- Myths: Do people commonly misunderstand this term, its meaning, or its usage? How?

- Alternatives: What are the synonyms for the term? What *accidental* synonyms exist?

When it comes to language, people are slow to change and quick to argue. Documenting these details will help you make your controlled vocabulary as clear and useful as possible.

Think about nouns and verbs.

Nouns represent each of the objects, people, and places involved in a mess.

As an example, a *post* is a noun commonly associated with another noun, an *author*.

Verbs represent the actions that can be taken.

A *post* (n.) can be: *written, shared, deleted,* or *read*.

Verbs don't exist without nouns. For example, an online *share* button implies that it will *share this post*.

Nouns are often created as a result of verbs. A *post* only exists after *posting*.

It's easy to adopt terms that are already in use or to be lazy in choosing our language. But when you're deciding which words to use, it is important to consider the alternatives, perceptions, and associations around each term.

How would your work be different if "authors writing posts" was changed to "researchers authoring papers," or "followers submitting comments?"

Think about relationships between nouns and verbs.

When you combine nouns with appropriate verbs, the resulting sentences can be referred to as **requirements** for what you're making.

From the previous example:

- An *author* can *write* a *post*.

- An *author* can *delete* a *post*.

- Any *user* can *share* a *post*.

- Any *user* can *read* a *post*.

This list of requirements defines the ideal solution. Each requirement tells us *who* should be able to do *what* in the eventual state.

When you take the time to make requirements concrete and prioritize them, you can better understand what you're actually making.

If you're designing an interface that prioritizes *reading*, it will be fundamentally different than an interface that prioritizes *writing*, even with the exact same list of requirements.

Watch out for options and opinions.

When we talk about what something has to do, we sometimes answer with **options** of what it *could* do or **opinions** of what it *should* do.

A strong requirement describes the results you want without outlining how to get there.

A weak requirement might be written as: "A user is able to easily publish an article with one click of a button." This simple sentence implies the interaction (one click), the interface (a button), and introduces an ambiguous measurement of quality (easily).

When we introduce implications and ambiguity into the process, we can unknowingly lock ourselves into decisions we don't mean to make.

As an example, I once had a client ask for a "homepage made of buttons, not just text." He had no idea that, to a web designer, a button is the way a user submits a form online. To my client, the word button meant he could change the content over time as his business changes.

Opinions are like…

No matter how hard we try to be aware of opinions swirling around us, it's hard to remain neutral. But in the end, progress can't happen without a decision.

When you're choosing a direction, you may run into these questions:

- What if I disagree with a user need or opinion identified in my research?

- What if I disagree with the way another stakeholder sees a core concept or decision?

- What if I don't want to do this the way others want me to?

Some people choose to hide from the realities behind these questions. But if you shield your ideas and simply follow orders, you may end up with goal-crushing (and soul-crushing) results.

We have to balance what we know with what we see and what other people say.

We listen to our users and our guts. There is no *one* right way. There is only *your* way.

Admit where you are.

Let's say you're on a weeklong bicycle trip. You planned to make it to your next stop before dark, but a flat tire delayed you by a few hours.

Even though you planned to get further along today, the truth is that pursuing that plan would be dangerous now.

Similarly, an idea you can draw on paper in one day may end up taking you a lifetime to make real. With the ability to make plans comes great responsibility.

Think about what you can do with the time and resources you have. Filtering and being realistic are part of the job. Keep reevaluating where you are in relation to where you want to go.

Be careful not to fall in love with your plans or ideas. Instead, fall in love with the effects you can have when you communicate clearly.

Meet Rasheed.

Rasheed is a consultant helping the human resources department of a large company. They want to move their employee-training processes online.

Rasheed's research uncovered a lot of language inconsistencies between how employees are hired and trained in various departments.

He always expects to account for departmental differences, but he fears this many similar terms for the same things will make for a sloppy system design.

Rasheed has a choice. He could document the terms as they exist and move on. Or he could take the time to find a direction that works for everyone.

He decides to group the terms by similar meanings and host a meeting with the departments to choose which terms should lead, and which ones should fall back.

During the meeting, Rasheed:

- Questions acronyms and proprietary terms

- Eliminates accidental synonyms

- Documents myths, alternatives, and histories

Control your vocabulary.

Are you facing a mess like Rasheed's? Do your stakeholders speak the same language? Do you collectively speak the same language as your users? What language might be troublesome in the context of what you are doing? What concepts need to be better understood or defined?

To control your vocabulary:

- Create a list of terms to explore.

- Define each term as simply as you can.

- Underline words within your definitions that need to be further defined, and define them.

- Document the history, alternatives, and myths associated with each term.

- Review your list of defined terms with some of your users. Refine the list based on their feedback.

- Create a list of requirements that join your nouns and verbs together.

Choose a direction.

WORDS WE SAY

TERM	DEFINITION	HISTORY

WORDS WE DON'T SAY

TERM	WHY NOT?	USE INSTEAD

REQUIREMENTS

NOUNS	ASSOCIATED VERBS

Download the worksheet at:
abbytheia.com/worksheets/direction.pdf

Tons
Miles
Duckets
Inches
Minutes
Hours
Distance
Pixels
Picas
Days
Months
Years
Seasons
Cycles
Strength

5

Measure the Distance

There's distance between reality and your intent.

Your intent shows you what you want to become when you're all grown up. But intent alone won't get things done.

Breaking your intent into specific goals helps you to figure out where to invest your time and energy, and how to measure your progress along the way.

A **goal** is something specific that you want to do. A well-defined goal has the following elements:

- Intent: What are the specific results you want to see for your efforts?

- Baseline: What points of reference can you use to compare your progress with where you are today?

- Progress: How will you measure movement towards or away from your goal?

Goals are our lens on the world.

Goals change what's possible and what happens next.

Whether big or small, for today or this year, goals change how you spend time and resources.

The ways you set and measure goals affects how you define a good day or a bad day, valuable partners or the competition, productive time or a waste of time.

Goals are only reachable when you're being realistic about the distance between reality and where you want to go. You may measure that distance in time, money, politics, talent, or technology.

Once you figure out the distance you need to travel, momentum can replace the anxiety of not knowing how to move forward.

Progress is as important to measure as success.

Many projects are more manageable if you cut them into smaller tasks. Sequencing those tasks can mean moving through a tangled web of dependencies.

A **dependency** is a condition that has to be in place for something to happen. For example, the links throughout this book are dependent on me publishing the content.

How you choose to measure progress can affect the likelihood of your success. Choose a measurement that reinforces your intent. For example:

- If you want to become a better writer, you might measure your progress against a goal like: "Write every day."

- If you want to write a novel in the next year, your progress may be better measured as: "Write 500 words towards the novel per day."

Indicators help us measure progress.

Most things can be measured by systems or people.

Indicators tell you if you're moving towards your intent or away from it. A business might use averages like dollars per order or call response time as indicators of how well they're doing.

It's not always easy to figure out how to measure things, but if you're persistent, you can gain invaluable insights about your progress.

The good news is the work it takes to define and measure indicators is almost always worth the effort.

To find the right indicators, start with these questions:

• What can you measure in your world?

• What could you measure if things changed?

• What signs would tell you if you're moving towards or away from your intent?

Examples of indicators follow on the next two pages.

Common indicators.

- Satisfaction: Are customers happy with what you're delivering against your promises?

- Kudos: How often do people praise you for your efforts or contributions?

- Profit: How much was left over after expenses?

- Value: What would someone pay for it?

- Loyalty: How likely are your users to return?

- Traffic: How many people used, visited, or saw what you made?

- Conversion: What percentage of people acted the way you hoped they would?

- Spread: How fast is word getting around about what you're doing?

- Perception: What do people believe about what you're making or trying to achieve?

- Competition: Who has similar intents to yours?

- Complaints: How many users are reaching out about an aspect of your product or service?

- Backlash: What negative commentary do you receive or expect?

- Expenses: How much did you spend?

- Debt: How much do you owe?

- Lost time: How many minutes, hours, or days did you spend unnecessarily?

- Drop-off: How many people leave without taking the action you hoped they would?

- Waste: How much do you discard, measured in materials and time?

- Murk: What alternative truths or opinions exist about what you're making or trying to achieve?

Use worksheets to mine data from people.

Once you have a list of indicators to guide you, think about where the data could come from.

A **worksheet** can help you capture important details that only exist in people's heads or personal records.

You can fill out a worksheet in a meeting or distribute copies of it and collect them after people have time to answer your questions. To choose the best way to gather the data, keep these considerations in mind:

- Time: How much are you asking for, and how long might it take?

- Access: How many sources are your respondents using to find answers? Who else might they need to contact?

- Bias: Are they applying their own thoughts and preferences, or delivering data?

If your users or stakeholders need a significant amount of time, access, or thought to answer your questions, let them get back to you instead of trying to get through the worksheet together.

Baselines help us stay in touch with reality.

The first step in understanding how something is performing is to measure it as it is.

A **baseline** is the measurement of something before changing it. Without baselines, assumptions will likely lead us in the wrong direction.

Here are two examples:

- If a prominent department store saw quarterly profits increase by $1.5M after their Super Bowl ad, the ad may be seen as effective. But if the baseline of regular quarterly profit increase for this brand is typically $5.5M+ after a Super Bowl ad, we'd judge the ad differently.

- Imagine an elementary school is reporting test scores averaging in the C+ range for the majority of their students. This may seem unimpressive, or even worrisome, until our baseline is introduced: average test scores this time last year were a D+.

When we have a baseline, we can judge performance. Without that, we may mistake the ad as successful and the teachers as incapable.

Flags tell us if we're headed in the right direction.

Flags are useful because they allow us to know when something important happens. We can attach a flag to most indicators.

These are all examples of flags:

- Having a loved one call when they arrive at their destination safely

- A dashboard light that reminds you to get gas in the next 50 miles

- A weekly email that shares customer service feedback with a design team

- An email alert when competitors are mentioned in the press

- A monthly report of how many users drop off at each step of an online registration process

Flags allow us to use data more proactively.

Measurements have rhythm.

Some things are best measured moment to moment. Others are best measured over weeks, months, years, or even decades.

The right rhythm depends on your context and your intent. When you're choosing a rhythm, think about the ways you collect data, how specific it needs to be, and how complex it is.

Consider these factors:

- Timeframe: Is this measurement most useful after one hour, one day, a season, a year, or an entire decade? What's a better baseline: yesterday, last month, a year ago, or twenty years ago?

- Access: Is the data readily available? Or does it require help from a particular person or system?

Fuzzy is normal.

What is good for one person can be profoundly bad for another, even if their goal is roughly the same. We each live within a unique set of contradictions and experiences that shape how we see the world.

Remember that there's no right or wrong way to do something. Words like *right* and *wrong* are subjective.

The important part is being honest about what you intend to accomplish within the complicated reality of your life. Your intent may differ from other people; you may perceive things differently.

You may be dealing with an indicator that's surprisingly difficult to measure, a data source that's grossly unreliable, or a perceptual baseline that's impossible to back up with data.

But as fuzzy as your lens can seem, setting goals with incomplete data is still a good way to determine if you're moving in the right direction.

Uncertainty comes up in almost every project. But you can only learn from those moments if you don't give up. Stick with the tasks that help you clarify and measure the distance ahead.

Meet Jim.

Jim owns a retail store. His profits and traffic have been declining for the last few years. His employees are convinced that, to save the business, the company website needs to let people buy things online. But all Jim sees is more complications, more people to manage, and more expenses. He thinks, "If we sell on the website, we have to take photos, and pack and ship each order. Who will do that?"

With rent going up and profits going down, Jim isn't sure if changing the website will save his business. He doesn't know the distance he needs to travel to get to his goal. He wonders, "Will improving my website even help? Or will it just make things worse?"

To think through this decision, Jim:

- Makes a list of indicators to measure the store

- Measures the baseline for each indicator

- Sets up flags that keep him informed of changes

- Identifies ways to improve towards his goals

If Jim's goal is to increase in-store traffic and reduce expenses, an online store probably doesn't make as much sense as other things he could do.

Set your goals.

Think about what you're trying to accomplish.

1. Revisit what you intend to do and why. Now break it down into specific goals.

2. Make a dream list of what would be measureable in an ideal world. Even if the measurement is fuzzy or hard to find, it's useful to think about the best-case scenario.

3. Remember to mine data from people.

4. Measure the baseline of what you can. Once you have your dream list, narrow it down to an achievable set of measurements to gather a baseline reading of.

5. Make a list of indicators to potentially measure.

6. List some situations where you'd want to be notified if things change. Then, figure out how to make those flags for yourself.

Measure the distance.

WHAT ARE YOU DOING?

I INTEND TO

BECAUSE

HOW WILL YOU KNOW IT WORKED?

INDICATOR	BASELINE	GOAL

WHAT FLAGS WOULD BE USEFUL?

TELL ME WHEN...	TELL ME WHEN...

Download the worksheet at:
abbytheia.com/worksheets/distance.pdf

Order
Scaffold
Construct
Configuration
Framing
Chassis
Formation
Structure
Organization
Categorization
Sorting
Skeleton
Corpus
Framework
Pile

6

Play with Structure

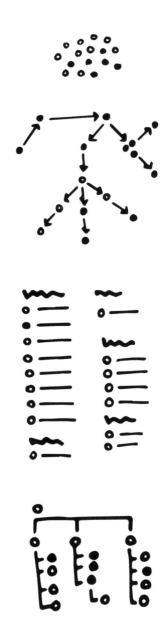

There are many ways to structure things.

A **structure** is a configuration. An unorganized pile is a structure. So is a table of contents or a house of cards. Every thing has a structure.

To choose a good structure for what you are making, you need to find one that:

- Makes sense to your users

- Reflects your intent

- Helps you to reach your goals

There will always be several structures you can use.

Allowing your content to try on a structure you believe to be bad or wrong can be helpful. When we determine what something *won't* be, we often reveal a little more about what it *will* be.

Don't settle for the first structure you come up with. Take the same things and arrange them, not in one way, but in two or three ways. Compare them. Iterate. Test. Refine. Combine. Change. Argue.

Taxonomy is how we arrange things.

When you set out to arrange something, how do you decide where the pieces go? Is it based on what looks right to you, what you believe goes together, or what someone told you to do? Or maybe you let gravity or the alphabet determine the order?

To effectively arrange anything, we have to choose methods for organizing and classifying content in ways that convey the intended information to our intended users.

Structural methods for organization and classification are called **taxonomy**.

Common examples of taxonomies include:

- The scientific classification for plants, animals, minerals, and other organisms

- The Dewey Decimal system for libraries

- Navigational tabs on a website

- Organizational charts showing management and team structures

We combine taxonomies to create unique forms.

Taxonomies shape our experience at every level. We use taxonomies to make sense of everything from systems to objects. It often takes multiple taxonomic approaches to make sense of a single form.

Form is the visual shape or configuration something takes. The form is what users actually experience.

Even a simple form like this book uses several taxonomies to help you read through the content, understand it, and use it.

A few taxonomies in this book:

- Table of contents

- Chapter sequence

- Page numbers

- Headlines that accompany brief expansions on an individual lesson

- An indexed lexicon

- Links to worksheets

Sorting is easier than deciding how to sort.

Sorting is the act of arranging content according to established rules. The act of deciding how to sort something within a taxonomy is called **classification**.

If you have a large pile of things, it may take a lot of time to sort through them. But sorting isn't the hard part. Classification is.

Think about sorting a bag of groceries into a pre-arranged pantry. Everything has a place. You're simply following the plan. Easy, right?

Now unload that same bag into a kitchen without rules for where things go. How much longer would it take you? How much more frustrating a task would it be? How much variation would you get when the next person unloads groceries?

Sorting is easy when clear rules are in place. But without those rules, assumptions take over and things end up in places where they can be harder to find.

The most challenging part of classification is working with other people to agree on a set of rules.

Classification can be exact or ambiguous.

Postal codes are what we call an **exact** classification. We can generally rely on the codes to hold steady. If the postal code is 10012, the building is in Manhattan. There's nothing to argue about. It just is.

Ambiguous classifications require more thought to decide where something goes. The more ambiguous something is, the more it can be argued about.

Movie genres like Comedy and Drama may seem exact. But if you put three movie reviewers in a room and ask them to classify a dark comedy into one of those two genres, they may challenge each other.

Ambiguity and exactness relate to context as well.

For example, in editing this book, Nicole suggested I use the term "Postal code" instead of "Zip code" in the example above. Both would have expressed the point, but one is more exact for our context, which includes readers outside of the United States.

Ambiguity costs clarity; exactitude costs flexibility.

The more ambiguous you are, the more likely it is that people will have trouble using your taxonomy to find and classify things.

For every ambiguous rule of classification you use or label you hide behind, you'll have to communicate your intent that much more clearly.

For example, what if I had organized the lexicon in the back of this book by chapter, instead of alphabetically? This might be an interesting way of arranging things, but it would need to be explained, so you could find a term.

The more exact your taxonomy becomes, the less flexible it is. This isn't always bad, but it can be. If you introduce something that doesn't fit into a category things can get confusing.

Because there are many words for the same thing, exact classifications can slow us down. For example, I recently tried to buy some zucchini at a grocery store. But it wasn't until the clerk in training found the code for "Squash, Green" that she could ring me up.

Ambiguity hides in simplicity.

Imagine that on your first day working at a record store, your manager says, "Our records are organized alphabetically." Under this direction, you file your first batch of vinyl with ease.

Later, you overhear a coworker saying, "Sorry, it looks like we're sold out of Michael Jackson right now."

Your manager looks under "J" and checks the inventory, which says the store should have a single copy of *Thriller*.

You remember that it was part of the shipment of records you just filed. Where else could you have put that record, if not under "J"? Maybe under "M"?

The ambiguity that's wrapped up in something as simple as "alphabetize these" is truly amazing.

We give and receive instructions all day long. Ambiguous instructions can weaken our structures and their trustworthiness. It's only so long after that first album is misfiled that chaos ensues.

Facets are the lenses we use to classify.

A **facet** is a discrete piece of knowledge you can use to classify something. The more facets something has, the more ways it can be organized.

Using the record store as an example, the following facets are available for each record:

- Record Name

- Artist Name

- Record Label

- Length

- Release Date

- Price

If a particular facet is interesting but the data to support it doesn't exist or is hard to gather, it might not be the best plan to use that facet.

For example, finding out which instrument models were used on each album may be interesting, but it is also likely to be quite time-consuming to collect.

Identify facets.

What are five other facets of a vinyl record?

1. _____

2. _____

3. _____

4. _____

5. _____

Consider:

- Which of these facets are most ambiguous?

- Which of these facets are most exact?

- Which of these facets would make sense for organizing a record store?

- Which of these facets would make sense for organizing a personal collection of records?

Now search Google for "John Cusack organizes records autobiographically" and think about the facets that Cusack's character would need to sort his collection that way.

Humans are complex.

Tomatoes are scientifically classified as a fruit. Some people know this and some don't. The tomato is a great example of the vast disagreements humans have with established exact classifications.

Our mental models shape our behavior and how we relate to information.

In the case of the tomato, there are clearly differences between what science classifies as a fruit and what humans consider appropriate for fruit salad.

If you owned an online grocery service, would you dare to only list tomatoes as fruit?

Sure, you could avoid the fruit or vegetable debate entirely by classifying everything as "produce," or you could list tomatoes in "fruit" and "vegetables."

But what if I told you that squash, olives, cucumbers, avocados, eggplant, peppers, and okra are also fruits that are commonly mistaken as vegetables?

What do we even mean when we say "fruit" or "vegetable" in casual conversations? Classification systems can be unhelpful and indistinguishable when you're sorting things for a particular context.

The way you organize things says a lot about you.

Classifying a tomato as a vegetable says something about what you know about your customers and your grocery store. You would classify things differently if you were working on a textbook for horticulture students, right?

How you choose to classify and organize things reflects your intent, but it can also reflect your worldview, culture, experience, or privilege.

Those same choices affect how people using your taxonomy understand what you share with them.

Taxonomies serve as a set of instructions for people interacting with our work.

Taxonomy is one of the strongest tools of rhetoric we have. The key to strong rhetoric is using language, rules and structures that your audience can easily understand and use.

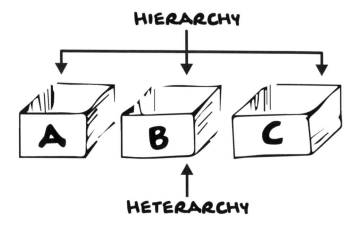

Taxonomies can be hierarchical or heterarchical.

When taxonomies are arranged **hierarchically**, it means that successive categories, ranks, grades, or interrelated levels are being used. In a hierarchy, a user would have to select a labeled grouping to find things within it. A hierarchy of movies might look like this:

- Comedies
  - Romantic comedies
  - Classic comedies
  - Slap-stick comedies

Hierarchies tend to follow two patterns. First, a **broad** and **shallow** hierarchy gives the user more choices up front so they can get to everything in a few steps. As an example, in a grocery store, you choose an aisle, and each aisle has certain arrangement of products, but that's as deep as you can go.

A **narrow** and **deep** hierarchy gives the user fewer choices at once. On a large website, like http://usa. gov, a few high level options point users to more specific items with each click.

When individual pieces exist on one level without further categorization, the taxonomy is **heterarchical**. For example, each lettered box in the arrangement on the previous page is heterarchical.

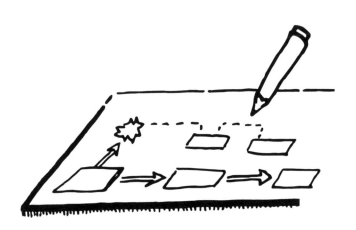

Taxonomies can be sequential.

Sequence is the order in which something is experienced. Some sequences happen in a logical order, where the steps are outlined ahead of time.

Other sequences are more complex with alternative paths and variations based on the circumstances, preferences, or choices of the user or the system.

These are all examples of sequences:

- A software installation wizard

- New patient sign-up forms

- A refund process at a retail store

- A job application

- A recipe

- A fiction book

- The checkout process on a website

Like any taxonomy, the categories and labels you choose affect how clear a sequence is to use.

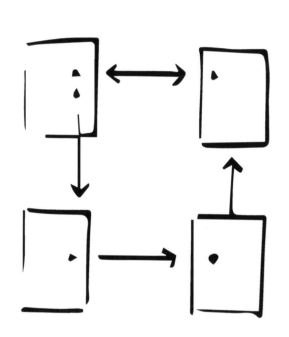

Hypertexts bridge taxonomies.

We use **hypertext** to connect things without necessarily placing them together.

Hypertexts are fundamentally different from hierarchical, heterarchical, and sequential taxonomies, because they don't change where things are located, just how they're found.

We use hyperlinks to allow users to jump between taxonomies instead of duplicating or moving content. For example, we might hyperlink the bolded words throughout this book. If a user clicks on one of them, we could take them to a definition in the lexicon. We're moving the user to the content instead of repeating it.

A signpost directing you to a store around the corner is also hypertextual, because it sends you to a specific location without changing the location of the store.

Similarly, websites use hypertext to link to content without needing to repeat it.

Most things need a mix of taxonomic approaches.

The world is organized in seemingly endless ways, but in reality, every form can be broken down into some taxonomic patterns.

Hierarchy, heterarchy, sequence, and hypertext are just a few common patterns. Most forms involve more than one of these.

A typical website has a hierarchical navigation system, a sequence for signing up or interacting with content, and hypertext links to related content.

A typical grocery store has a hierarchical aisle system, a heterarchical database for the clerk to retrieve product information by scanning a barcode, and sequences for checking out and other basic customer service tasks. I was even in a grocery store recently where each cart had a list of the aisle locations of the 25 most common products. A great use of hypertext.

A typical book has a sequence-based narrative, a hierarchical table of contents, and a set of facets allowing it to be retrieved with either the Dewey Decimal system at a library, or within a genre-based hierarchical system used in bookstores and websites like Amazon.com.

Meet Joan.

Joan is the social media coordinator for an airline that recently merged with another airline. Overnight, her team became responsible for twice as much work as before. She's also now responsible for managing twice as many people.

As the details of the merger iron out, duplicative channels have to be dealt with. For example, they now have two Twitter accounts and two help directories on two different websites. To tie everything together, Joan:

- Conducts user and stakeholder research

- Develops a controlled vocabulary to identify the nouns and verbs of both companies across their existing channels

- States the intent of each channel and determines the best direction to serve users

- Develops specific goals and baselines

- Identifies a set of flags to keep her informed

- Maps out the channels that she manages and how the merger will affect each over time

- Organizes each channel to better serve stakeholders and users

Play with structure.

Because your structure may change a hundred times before you finish making it, you can save time and frustration by thinking with boxes and arrows before making real changes. Boxes and arrows are easier to move around than the other materials we work with, so start there.

Try structuring the mess with common patterns of boxes and arrows as shown on the next page. Remember that you'll probably need to combine more than one pattern to find a structure that works.

1. Assess the content and facets that are useful for what you're trying to convey.

2. Play with broad and shallow versus narrow and deep hierarchies. Consider the right place to use heterarchies, sequences, and hypertext arrangements.

3. Arrange things one way and then come up with another way. Compare and contrast them. Ask other people for input.

4. Think about the appropriate level of ambiguity or exactitude for classifying and labeling things within the structure you're pursuing.

Learn these patterns.

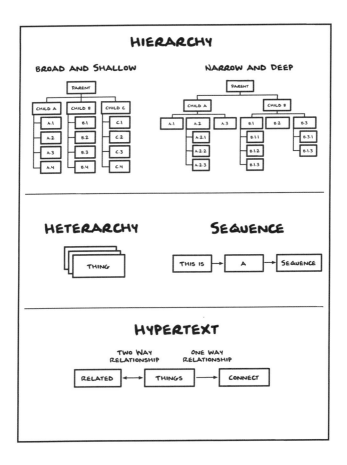

Download the worksheet at:
abbytheia.com/worksheets/structure.pdf

Adapt
Modify
Edit
Resolve
Reorient
Blowup
Startover
Adjust
Change
Rearrange
Tweak
Flex
Pivot
Swerve

7

Prepare to Adjust

Adjustments are a part of reality.

From moment to moment, the directions we choose forever change the objects we make, the effects we see, and the experiences we have.

As we move towards our goals, things change and new insights become available. Things always change when we begin to understand what we couldn't make sense of before. As a sensemaker, the most important skill you can learn is to adjust your course to accommodate new forces as you encounter them on your journey.

Don't seek finalization. Trying to make something that will never change can be super frustrating. Sure, it's work to move those boxes and arrows around as things change. But that is *the* work, not a reason to avoid making a plan. Taking in feedback from other people and continuously refining the pieces as well as the whole is what assures that something is "good."

Don't procrastinate. Messes only grow with time. You can easily make excuses and hold off on doing something until the conditions are right, or things seem stable.

Perfection isn't possible, but progress is.

The sum is greater than its parts.

We need to understand the sum of a lot of pieces to make sense of what we have.

For example, let's say we're working on bringing a product to the market. To support this process, we might create:

- A hierarchical diagram of how the product is structured and labeled for users

- A flow diagram of the sequence users experience in the product

- A lexicon of terms the product will use, vetted to make sense to our audience

These are all important pieces individually, but we need to look at them together to answer questions about the whole such as:

- What will users experience?

- Who will work on what, why, and with whom?

- When will things be released and how?

- How will things change over time?

It's easy to reach agreement alone.

Maybe you're working on a project independently and you're the only stakeholder and user.

More likely, you're working with other people to serve other people. In that scenario, making maps and diagrams alone at your desk is not practicing information architecture.

Your whole team should be able to influence and react to your tools and methods. You should be making prototypes to get feedback from users on language and structure.

Getting everyone involved early is crucial. Every step you take should come from the direction you choose together. If you don't get agreement up front, prepare for more work later.

When you see the world through the eyes of other people, you can spot weaknesses and opportunities for improvement. Don't hide from other stakeholders or wait until the end of the project to talk to users.

~~Argue about~~ discuss it until it's clear.

It's totally normal for fear, anxiety, and linguistic insecurity to get in the way of progress. Learning to work with others while they're experiencing these not-so-pleasant realities is the hardest part of making sense of a mess.

Tension can lead to arguments. Arguments can cause resentment. Resentment can kill momentum. And when momentum stalls, messes grow larger and meaner.

To get through the tension, try to understand other people's positions and perceptions:

- How does this mess look to them?

- What does their mental model look like?

- What words do they use? Could your language mislead them?

- Do they agree with the intent, direction, and goals you outlined?

- Do they agree on the level you're working at?

If it isn't under the floorboards, it's a façade.

Information architecture is like the frame and foundation of a building. It's not a building by itself, but you can't add the frame and foundation after the building is up. They're critical parts of the building that affect the whole of it. Buildings without frames do not exist.

It's hard to relay your intended meaning through façade alone. When your structure and intent don't line up, things fall apart.

Imagine trying to open a fancy restaurant in an old Pizza Hut. The shape of its former self persists in the structure. The mid-nineties nostalgia for that brand is in its bones. Paint the roof; change the signage; blow out the inside; it doesn't matter. The building insists, "I used to be a Pizza Hut."

(Now type "used to be Pizza Hut" into Google's image search and enjoy the laugh riot!)

We serve many masters.

No matter what the mess is made of, we have many masters, versions of reality, and needs to serve. Information is full of history and preconceptions.

Stakeholders need to:

- Know where the project is headed

- See patterns and potential outcomes

- Frame the appropriate solution for users

Users need to:

- Know how to get around

- Have a sense of what's possible based on their needs and expectations

- Understand the intended meaning

It's our job to uncover subjective reality.

An important part of that is identifying the differences between what stakeholders think users need and what users think they need for themselves.

Make room for information architecture.

If you find yourself needing to promote this practice, here are some ways you can talk about it:

You: "Wow, we have lots of information floating around about this, huh?"

Them: "It's a bit unruly, isn't it?"

You: "Yeah, I think I can help though. I recently learned about the practice of information architecture. Have you heard of it?

Them: "Never heard of it. What is it?"

You: "It's the practice of deciding which structures we need so our intent comes through to users."

Them: "Is it hard? Do we need an expert?"

You: "Well, it isn't hard if we're willing to collaborate and make decisions about what we're doing. I have some tools we can try. What do you think?"

"Hey, nice IA!" said no one, ever.

No one comments on the plumbing or electricity of a building unless the toilet is clogged or the lights aren't working. Then all of a sudden, pipes and wires are a hot topic of conversation.

Similarly, people don't compliment or even critique information architecture unless it's broken.

The "information architecture part" is almost invisible when separated from how something looks and how it's made. For example, we can't evaluate the quality of the structure of this book without considering how it was written, edited, designed, illustrated, typeset, manufactured, and delivered.

If you practice information architecture for the glory, get ready to be disappointed.

But if you practice it for the clarity it can bring, get ready for some seriously interesting work.

Be the filter, not the grounds.

When making a cup of coffee, the filter's job is to get the grit out before a user drinks the coffee. Sensemaking is like removing the grit from the ideas we're trying to give to users.

What we remove is as important as what we add. It isn't just the ideas that get the work done.

Be the one *not* bringing the ideas. Instead, be the filter that other people's ideas go through to become drinkable:

- Shed light on the messes that people see but don't talk about.

- Make sure everyone agrees on the intent behind the work you're doing together.

- Help people choose a direction and define goals to track your progress.

- Evaluate and refine the language and structures you use to pursue those goals.

With those skills, you'll always have people who want to work with you.

This is hard.

It's hard to decide to tear down a wall, take off the roof, or rip up the floorboards. It's hard to admit when something architectural isn't serving you.

It's hard to find the words for what's wrong.

It's hard to deal with the time between understanding something is wrong and fixing it.

It's hard to get there.

It's hard to be honest about what went right and what went poorly in the past.

It's hard to argue with people you work with about fuzzy things like meaning and truth.

It's hard to ask questions.

It's hard to hear criticism.

It's hard to start over.

It's hard to get to good.

It's far more *rewarding* than hard.

It's rewarding to set a goal and reach it.

It's rewarding to know that you're communicating in a language that makes sense to others.

It's rewarding to help someone understand something in a way they hadn't before.

It's rewarding to see positive changes from the insights you gather.

It's rewarding to know that something is good.

It's rewarding to give the gifts of clarity, realistic expectations, and clear direction.

It's rewarding to make this world a little clearer.

It's rewarding to make sense of the messes you face.

Meet Abby.

Abby Covert is an **information architect**. After ten years of practicing information architecture for clients, Abby worried that too few people knew how to practice it themselves. She decided that the best way to help would be to teach this important practice.

After two years of teaching without a textbook, Abby told her students that she intended to write the book that was missing from the world: a book about information architecture for everybody.

As she wrote the first draft, she identified a mess of inconsistencies in the language and concepts inherent in teaching an emerging practice. At the end of the semester, she had a textbook for art school students, but she didn't have the book that she intended to write for everybody. She had gone in the wrong direction to achieve a short-term goal.

She was frustrated and fearful of starting over. But instead of giving up, Abby faced her reality and used the advice in this book to make sense of her mess.

To get to the book you now hold, she wrote over 75,000 words, defined over 100 terms as simply as she could, and tested three unique prototypes with her users.

She hopes that it makes sense.

Make sense yet?

1. Have you explored the depth and edges of the mess that you face?

2. Do you know why you have the intent you have and what it means to how you will solve your problem?

3. Have you faced reality and thought about contexts and channels your users could be in?

4. What language have you chosen to use to clarify your direction?

5. What specific goals and baselines will you measure your progress against?

6. Have you put together various structures and tested them to make sure your intended message comes through to users?

7. Are you prepared to adjust?

Resources.

To learn more about the practice of information architecture, check out these resources:

Books

Robert Gushko, *The Discipline of Organization*
Heather Hedden, *The Accidental Taxonomist*
Andrew Hinton, *Understanding Context*
Kevin Lynch, *An Image of the City*
Peter Morville, *Interwingled*
Andrea Resmini, *Reframing IA*
Nathan Shedroff, *Design is the Problem*
Donna Spencer, *Card Sorting*
Edward Tufte, *Visual Explanations*
Richard Saul Wurman, *Information Anxiety II*
Indi Young, *Mental Models*

Websites

BoxesAndArrows.com
IAInstitute.org
iA.net/blog
Semanticstudios.com
Understandinggroup.com

Indexed lexicon.

This is the controlled vocabulary for this book. It's not exhaustive; it focuses on ontological decisions that went into my writing. For more information, visit: abbytheia.com/lexicon

Ambiguous (adj.): *69, 100, 129 -133*	Open to interpretation.
Architect (v.): *15, 16, 20, 23, 55*	To determine the structure of something.
Baseline (n.): *108, 115, 117-120, 143, 160*	A measurement of something before making changes.
Block Diagram (n.): *66, 76*	A diagram depicting how objects and their attributes interrelate to create a concept.
Broad (adj.): *137, 144, 145*	Provides many choices at once.
Channel (n.): *53, 54, 73, 78, 87, 143, 160*	Anything that carries or transfers information.
Choreograph (v.): *86*	To determine the sequence of steps and movements users can take.
Classification (n.): *126, 128, 129, 130, 132, 134, 135, 144*	The process of sorting things with similar qualities or characteristics. *See also: Classify (v.)*

Communication (n.): *11, 16, 20, 33, 38, 41, 61, 88, 102, 130*	The act of transmitting thoughts, messages, or information to people or systems. See *also: Communicate* (v.)
Concept (n.): *20, 63, 66, 70, 72, 73, 76, 89-95, 101, 104, 159*	An abstract idea or general notion.
Condition (n.): *67, 110, 148*	The relative state of something.
Connection (n.): *17, 67, 73, 84, 96, 141*	A relationship or association that links a person, thing, or idea with another person, thing, or idea. *See also: Connectivity (n.) & Connect (v.)*
Content (n.): *21, 23, 27, 28, 63, 76, 100, 110, 125-128, 141, 142, 144*	Things that are being arranged or sequenced.
Context (n.): *53-55, 73, 75, 78, 87, 89, 90, 92, 95, 104, 117, 118, 129, 134, 160*	The surroundings, circumstances, environments, background, and settings that determine, specify, or clarify the meaning of an event or other occurrence. *See also: Contextual (adj.)*
Controlled Vocabulary (n.): *93, 94, 97, 143, 162*	An organized list of terms, phrases, and concepts to help someone understand a topic or domain.
Data (n.): *17, 21, 28, 69, 114, 116-118, 120, 132*	A collection of facts, observations, and questions about something.

Deep (adj.): *137, 144*	A structure with many nested levels of classification.
Dependency (n.): *110*	A condition that must be in place for something to occur.
Design (v.): *61, 63, 64, 92, 99, 155,*	To plan something with an intended outcome. *See also: Designed (adj.)*
Diagram (n.): *57-67, 69, 7-74, 76, 78, 79, 143, 149, 150*	Any illustration or picture that helps an audience understand something.
Direction (n.): *17, 40, 41, 81, 82, 88, 101, 103, 105, 109, 115, 116, 118, 131,143, 148, 150, 151, 156, 158-160*	An indication of the place something or someone is traveling toward.
Ecosystem (n.): *84*	A collection of interrelated systems.
Exact (adj.): *24, 43, 69, 129, 130, 133, 134, 144*	A precise way of classifying things. *See also: Exactly (adv.), Exactness (n.), Exactitude (n)*
Exploded Schematic (n.): *74*	A diagram that shows how its pieces come together to create a whole.
Form (n.): *65, 74, 127, 142*	Whatever is created when content is sorted into a structure for use.
Façade (n.): *152*	The visible face of something.

Facet (n.): *132, 133, 142, 144*	Any aspect, piece of knowledge, or feature that can be used to sort or retrieve something
Flag (n.): *116, 119, 120, 143*	A prescribed circumstance in which data is delivered.
Flow Diagram (n.): *67, 76, 149*	A diagram depicting the steps in a discrete process, including conditions, connections, and places related to it.
Frame (v.): *65, 152, 153*	To arrange or adjust for a specific purpose. *See also: Frame (n.), Framing (n.)*
Gantt Chart (n.): *68, 76*	A diagram depicting a process or set of processes as they relate to one another step-by-step over time.
Goal (n.): *16, 101, 108 - 110, 118-120, 125, 143, 148, 151, 156, 158-160*	A desired result.
Heterarchy (n.): *137, 141, 142, 145*	A classification method in which the individual pieces exist without rank, or level. *See also: heterarchical (adj.)*
Hierarchy (n.): *72, 73, 76, 137, 142, 145, 149*	A classification method that applies successive ranks and levels. *See also: hierarchical (adj.), hierarchy diagram (n.)*

Homograph (n.): *33, 94*	A term that has different meanings depending on its context.
How (n.): *12, 15, 17, 20, 23, 24, 28, 32, 33, 35, 37-45, 53, 54, 60, 63, 64, 66, 68 - 72, 74, 76, 82, 85, 86, 94, 97, 98, 100, 101, 103, 108-118, 120, 126, 128, 134, 135, 139, 141, 143, 149, 151, 153, 155, 159, 160*	The specific ways something will be made or delivered.
Hypertext (n.): *141, 142, 144, 145*	When things are arranged so that related items are connected through an action taken by a user. *See also: Hypertextual (adj.)*
Indicator (n.): *111-114, 116, 118-121*	A measurement or event used to monitor the operation or condition of something.
Information (n.): *11-15, 16, 19, 20, 21, 23, 26, 28, 34, 53, 55, 64, 95, 126, 134, 142, 150, 152, 153, 154, 155*	Whatever is intrepreted from a particular arrangement or sequence of things. *See also: inform (v.)*
Information Architecture (n.): *13, 15, 19, 26, 34, 95, 150, 152, 154, 155, 159, 161*	**As an object:** The way we arrange the parts of something to make it more understandable as a whole. **As a practice:** The act of deciding how pieces of a whole should be arranged to best communicate to intended users.
Information Architect (n.): *95, 159*	A person who helps other people determine or improve their information architecture.

Intent (n.): *20, 23, 32, 39, 41, 43 - 47, 51, 86, 94, 108, 109, 110, 111, 113, 117, 118, 125, 130, 135, 143, 151, 154, 156, 160*	The planned meaning and outcomes.
Interface (n.): *74, 84, 99, 100*	A point where a user affects a location or object.
Interpretation (n.): *17, 18, 20, 21, 23, 24, 27, 28, 33, 37,*	A mental representation of the meaning of something. See also: *Interpret (v.), Interpreted (adj), Interpreting (v.)*
Journey (n.): *12, 75, 76, 84, 148*	The steps taken within or between locations. *See also: Journey Map (n.)*
Knowledge (n.): *12, 18, 20, 24, 26 -28, 35, 39, 40, 41, 43, 50, 52, 86, 57, 77, 82, 85, 91, 92*	Familiarity, awareness, or understanding gained through experience and study. *See also: Knowing (v.), Know (n.), Know (v.)*
Language (n.): *20, 28, 32 - 34, 44, 46, 55, 88, 89, 92, 93, 96-98, 103, 104, 135, 150, 151, 156, 158, 159, 160*	A system for communicating.
Lexicography (n.): *90*	The collection of varied meanings for single terms. *See also: Lexicon (n.)*
Linguistic Insecurity (n.): *89, 151*	The feeling of anxiety, self-consciousness, or lack of confidence surrounding the use of language in a specific context.
Location (n.): *84, 90, 141*	A particular place or position.

Map (n.): *57, 59, 60, 61, 65, 72, 73, 75 -78, 91, 150*	A diagram that shows how places are arranged within a defined area.
Matrix Diagram (n.): *78*	A diagram outlining differentiated areas for sorting, presentation, discussion, or definition of ideas.
Meaning (n.): *18, 26, 33, 34, 37, 38, 45, 52, 78, 90, 94-97, 100, 103, 110, 112, 134, 137, 151, 152, 153, 157, 160*	The perceived significance, understanding, or importance of something.
Mental Model (n.): *57, 77, 94, 134, 151*	The internal belief structure and thought process we use to make sense of the world.
Mess (n.): *11, 12, 15-19, 25-29, 33-38, 41, 50, 51, 54, 87, 64, 65, 78, 90, 98, 104, 144, 148, 151, 153, 156, 158, 159, 160*	A situation where the interactions between people and information are confusing or full of difficulties.
Mind Map (n.): *73, 75, 76*	A diagram depicting connections between concepts, objects, ideas, channels, people, and places within a particular context that don't necessarily live under an established hierarchy or sequence.
Narrow (n.): *137, 144, 145*	A structure with fewer choices at once.
Noun (n.): *98, 99, 104, 105, 143*	A person, place, or thing.

Object (n.): *20, 56-59, 66, 70, 72-74, 76, 84, 98, 127, 148, 153*	A material thing that can be seen or touched. *See also: Objective (adj.). Object of Discourse (n.)*
Ontology (n.): *90-92*	The declaration of meaning for terms and concepts within a specific context. *See also: ontological (adj.)*
Opinion (n.): *25, 33, 100, 101, 113*	A personal belief or view about something.
Option (n.): *25, 32, 41, 61, 100, 137*	A possible way forward.
Perception (n.): *17, 33, 37, 57, 98, 112, 118, 151*	The process of considering, understanding, and interpreting something. *See also: Perceive (v.)*
Place (n.): *17, 72, 73, 75, 83, 84, 86, 87, 98, 110, 128*	A portion of space designated for a purpose.
Placemaking (n.): *86*	The act of determining how to communicate the intended purpose of a place to its users.
Progress (n.): *25, 28, 82, 101, 108, 110, 111, 148, 151, 156, 160*	Movement toward a direction.
Purpose (n.): *59, 65, 87, 90, 125*	The reason why something is done.
Quadrant Diagram (n.): *69, 76*	A diagram that depicts how a group of things compare to one another according to either exact or ambiguous spectrums of classification.

Reality (n.): *26, 35, 50-55, 57, 61, 77-79, 82, 108, 109, 115, 118, 142, 148, 153, 159, 160*	The experiences that determine how things appear to a person.
Relationship (n.): *35, 63, 68, 72, 90, 99*	A connection between things.
Requirement (n.): *99, 100, 104, 105*	Something that's needed or wanted.
Rhetoric (n.): *61, 135*	Communication designed to have a persuasive effect on its audience.
Scale (n.): *59, 60*	The relative size of something.
Schematic (n.): *74, 76*	A representation of an object or interface.
Scope (n.): *59, 60, 103*	The areas and requirements that are included in the work being done.
Sequence (n.): *19, 20, 86, 73, 127, 142, 144, 149*	The order in which things are encountered.
Shallow (adj.): *137, 144*	A structure with only a few nested levels of classification.
Sitemap (adj.): *72*	A hierarchical diagram representing the relationships between pages or page states on a website.
Space (adj.): *86, 87*	An area that is free, available, or unoccupied.

Stakeholder (n.): *25, 27, 28, 34, 38, 51, 64, 88, 93, 94, 101, 104, 114, 143, 144, 150, 153*	Someone with a viable and legitimate interest in the work that you're doing.
Structure (n.): *11, 13, 16, 55, 63, 84, 90, 125, 126, 131, 135, 14, 144, 145, 149, 150, 152, 154,-156, 160*	A configuration of objects.
Subjective (adj.): *18, 20, 33, 37, 153*	Particular to an individual.
Swin Lane Diagram (n.): *71, 76*	A diagram depicting how multiple users work together within a system.
Synonym (n.): *93, 97, 103*	A term that closely resembles another word or phrase in meaning.
System (n.): *13, 15, 17, 33, 55, 60, 67, 84, 102, 111, 117, 126, 127, 134, 139, 142*	A set of structures.
Taxonomy (n.): *126, 127, 130, 135, 137, 139, 142*	The classification of something.
Timescale (n.): *60*	The period of time represented by a diagram or map.
Thing (n.): *11-13, 15-21, 23, 24, 32-39, 43, 44, 46, 50, 53, 54, 60, 61, 63, 64, 66, 69, 70, 72, 82-87, 89, 92, 94, 100, 108, 110, 111, 115-120, 125- 132, 134, 135, 137, 139, 141-144, 148, 149, 152, 155, 157, 158*	A separate or self-contained entity. *See also: Everything (n.), Anything (n.), Nothing (n.)*
Truth (n.): *18, 21, 23, 28, 33, 41, 102, 113, 155*	An accepted belief. *See also: True (adj.)*

User (n.): *20, 24, 27-29, 34, 35, 38, 45-47, 51, 53, 54, 61, 67, 71, 76, 78, 83, 84, 86-88, 93, 94, 95, 98, 99-101, 104, 112-114, 116, 125-127, 137, 139, 141, 143, 144, 149, 150, 153, 154, 156, 159, 160*	A person who encounters a message.
Venn Diagram (n.): *70, 76*	A diagram depicting the result of overlapping concepts or objects.
Verb (n.): *98, 99, 104, 105, 143*	An action, state, or occurrence.
What (n.): *16-21, 24, 26-28, 33, 34, 38-40, 43, 45, 46, 50-55, 57, 59, 63, 64, 76, 77, 78, 82, 84-85, 88-93, 97, 99-104, 108, 109, 111-114, 117, 118, 120, 125-130, 133-135, 144, 148, 149, 151, 153-157, 160*	The thing or things that specify something.
Why (n.): *24, 28, 33, 39, 41, 43, 82, 92, 95, 120, 149, 160*	The reason or explanation for something.
Worksheet (n.): *114, 127*	Any object made to capture answers to questions.

Thank you.

Rick, Liz, and Sydney Covert, for making me who I am.

James Sanford, for loving me as I am.

Bill & Ethel Pink, for teaching me to always be clear.

Tess Kisner, for always being there.

Dan Klyn, for letting me stand on your shoulders.

Carl Collins, for watching the scales fall from my eyes and never ripping them off early.

Caleb Brown, for teaching me to believe in my sensemaking abilities far before I knew I had any.

Andrew Hinton, for bringing me into the IA community.

Michael Leis, for teaching me to never feed the trolls.

Peter Morville, for making so much darn sense.

Lou Rosenfeld, for all the things he helped to start that make my life what it is today and for all his guidance.

Christina Wodtke, for teaching me to optimize for joy.

Thank you.

Nicole Fenton, for making every word I wrote better.

Allan Chochinov, for believing in my idea of teaching Information Architecture to everyone in the world.

Jorge Arango, for always asking why.

Joe Elmendorf, for putting clarity first always.

Kaarin Hoff, for being so thoughtful and kind in your feedback on my writing and ideas.

Michael Adcock, for giving me confidence in this bold approach and encouraging me to think harder.

Nick Senior, for listening to me whine.

Samantha Raddatz, for being ready to take on messes.

The Dublin Corp, for the thoughtful email banter.

The Jo's Gang, for all of the things.

My students, for whom I sought these answers.